The Official
Leeds
United
Annual 2013

CW00734964

Written by John Wray

Photography:
Andrew Varley Picture Agency

Great Northern Books
PO Box 213, Ilkley, LS29 9WS
www.greatnorthernbooks.co.uk

Design and layout: David Burrill

ISBN: 978-1905080-24-3

CIP Data
A catalogue for this book is available from the British Library

GREAT NORTHERN

£7.99

Contents

No better place to start your career...

THROUGHOUT his career, first as a player and then as a manager, Neil Warnock has possessed a burning desire to succeed and prove people wrong.

So the Leeds United manager is quick to reassure youngsters looking to make their way in the game that opportunities are there, even if things don't quite work out the first time around.

Players like Aidy White and Tom Lees have come through the Academy system to earn first team status at Elland Road, while many youngsters who have left the club have received the high quality coaching that has equipped them to build a career in the game elsewhere.

The England team's failure to win a major tournament since the 1966 World Cup is often blamed on the high number of foreign players in our game, but even outside the Premier League there are opportunities for home-grown players to make a very comfortable living for themselves – if they have the talent and work ethic everyone needs to succeed.

In fact, it is often better for any youngster with ambitions to play at the highest level, to start with a club outside the top flight where the chances of breaking into the first team are much greater.

As Neil says: "Football is a great game, and looking around at the Leeds United Academy, there is no better place to start. I have seen all the age groups here and they are receiving excellent coaching. If you are good enough you will be involved in one of the teams and the chance is there to make it all the way into the first team.

"I have encouraged youngsters and looked to bring them through at all my clubs. The fans love to see young lads like Aidy and Tom. They can relate to those players and always give them a bit of extra support.

"When I was at Crystal Palace we had a fantastic Academy. For those kids, making it as a footballer was the be-all and end-all. You became a footballer or you had nothing in life. I can honestly say I haven't found that hunger anywhere else in the country. They were desperate for opportunities and I gave about 16 of them their debuts in about 18 months!

"It has been good to see many of Palace's youngsters come through like Victor Moses, Nathaniel Clyne and Dazet Zaha."

Neil may be one of the game's longest serving managers, with a host of credits to his name, but he admits that during his 13-year playing career he was "just an average winger."

He said: "I must confess I wasn't good enough to know for certain that I was going to get a contract every year. Every February or March I used to worry about maybe getting a free transfer. I had a couple of those, but I was still determined to make a living out of the game.

"If you start out at a place like Leeds and fail, it's not the end of the world. I've seen so many good young players leave Football League clubs for non-league and then fight their way back at 21 or 22 years of age. There is always the opportunity to do well if you are good enough and have the right attitude."

One of the worst jobs Neil has to do as a manager is to tell youngsters they are not being kept on, and he knows from experience how soul-destroying that can be for the lads being shown the door. At Chesterfield he found out he wasn't being offered a contract when someone phoned him and told him it was in the newspaper.

"That was a terrible way to find out and I cried my eyes out," he recalled. "You live and learn, so with that experience in mind I've always made sure during my time as a manager that my players are the first to know about important decisions like that. It is the same with team sheets. I always tell the players the team first."

In all sport, though, there have to be winners and losers, but Neil says: "Always remember that taking part is very important, as well as doing your best and improving. Doing your best is all you can do, as a player and as a coach. All through my career, as a player and manager, I have tried to prove people wrong and that has spurred me on."

WHEN El-Hadji Diouf first arrived at Elland Road there were raised eyebrows among Leeds fans who, to put it mildly, didn't count the Senegalese striker or winger among their most liked footballers.

But the man who was booed by home supporters when he made his Elland Road debut as a substitute in the 4-0 win over Shrewsbury Town in the Capital One Cup first round on August 11, 2012, went on to win over his critics with some excellent displays in the white shirt.

Diouf played for Sochaux, Rennes and Lens before joining Liverpool for £10 million in 2002. He went on to join Bolton, Sunderland, Blackburn, Rangers (on loan) and Doncaster Rovers before arriving at Leeds on trial. He scored his first goal for United in the 3-3 draw against one of his old clubs Blackburn on September 1 and after the game he agreed a contract designed to keep him at Elland Road until January, 2013, at least.

El-Hadji Diouf

Easy and Not so Easy

1 Easy:
Who was Leeds United's top scorer in the 2011-12 season?

2 Not quite so easy:
How many Championship goals did he score?

3 Easy:
What is the name of Leeds United's ground?

4 Not quite so easy:
Which visiting team attracted our highest attendance during the 2011-12 season?

5 Easy:
Striker Luciano Becchio was born in which country?

6 Not quite so easy:
In which year did he join Leeds United?

7 Easy:
Goalkeeper Paddy Kenny joined us from which club in the summer of 2012?

8 Not quite so easy:
Which country did he play for?

9 Easy:
Which former Leeds United manager's statue stands opposite the East Stand and was unveiled last season?

10 Not quite so easy:
For what team did he play when he was made Footballer of the Year?

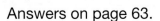

Answers on page 63.

Andy Gray

In the Family

WHEN your dad is Frank Gray and your uncle is Eddie Gray, people are sure to make comparisons, whether you like it or not.

Which is hardly fair when you consider the dizzy heights Frank and Eddie scaled for Leeds United and Scotland over the years.

Living in the shadow of his famous father and uncle is something Andy Gray has long had to live with, yet he is just happy to have carved out an enjoyable career of his own with eleven clubs.

"Having Frank as my dad and Eddie as my uncle hasn't been a monkey on my back at all," he insists. "I don't see it that way. They were both very good footballers in their own right. Fortunately I've had a decent career myself, though obviously not as good as them. I don't want to compare myself with them because it wouldn't be fair.

"They have both been a great help to me over the years. Although they've never pushed me, they have always been there to offer advice when I needed it. We speak regularly anyway and always talk a lot about football."

Dad Frank had two spells at Leeds, where he was a first division title winner in 1973-4. He also tasted success at Nottingham Forest, where he won the European Cup and the European Super Cup under Brian Clough's management. Having appeared in the 1974 European Cup Final, when Leeds were defeated by Bayern Munich in Paris, Frank's appearance with Forest made him the first player to play in the final for two different English clubs and he won 32 caps for Scotland.

Eddie, who played with distinction for United between 1965 and 1983, making 454 appearances and scoring 52 goals, was a mesmerising winger who many believe would have been as good as George Best if he had suffered fewer injuries, which restricted his Scotland caps to just 12.

Eddie won the League Cup, FA Cup, Fairs Cup and League Championship with Leeds and managed the club from 1982 to 1985. He was also caretaker-manager in 2003-4.

Harrogate-born Andy started out as a youngster at Elland Road, having joined the club from school, and he went on to turn out for Forest, Bury, Preston, Oldham, Bradford City, Sheffield United, Sunderland, Burnley, Charlton and Barnsley before Neil Warnock took him back to Leeds where it all began.

In his first spell at the club, Andy played in midfield and was outstanding in the 1996 League Cup Final against Aston Villa, though United went down to a 3-0 defeat. Many Leeds fans rate that as his best performance for the club, but he recalls a game at Old Trafford in April, 1996, and says modestly, "I did all right in that game too."

Watched by a crowd of over 48,000, Leeds had goalkeeper Mark Beeney sent off after only 17 minutes, Lucas Radebe taking over the gloves and keeping his goal intact until Roy Keane

scored the only goal in the 72nd minute.

After going out on loan to Bury, Andy was sold to fellow Premier League side Nottingham Forest but further loan spells came at Oldham and Preston before his permanent switch into a striker role at Bradford City.

"Somebody at Bradford was injured so I went up front and I've played in that position ever since," said Andy. "When Paul Hart was the youth team coach at Leeds he told me I would end up playing as a striker, but it never happened in my first spell with the club. Paul was proved right."

Andy scored 20 league goals in 77 games for Bradford and was named their Player of the Year in 2003. Recalling his time with the Bantams, he said: "I enjoyed it there, though it was a hard time for the club because they had just been relegated from the Premier League and were going into administration before I left.

"There was a really good spirit at the club and there were a lot of good players left over from the Premier League days."

After Neil Warnock signed him for Sheffield United, Andy returned to the Premier League with Sunderland, went on loan to Burnley and Charlton before his Charlton move became permanent and then joined Barnsley where he helped the Tykes to that 5-2 thrashing of Simon Grayson's side at Oakwell in September, 2010.

Now he says: "It's great to be back at Leeds. Ever since I left I've wanted to come back. I had worked with the manager (Neil Warnock) at Sheffield United, we got in touch with each other and he said 'come in and we will take a look at you to see if you are still fit and we will just take it from there.' I came in for training and he decided he would like to sign me.

"A lot of water has flowed under the bridge since I left and now that I'm back I just want to play as many games as I can and try to help. I know I am not going to be playing every week but I would like to contribute in other ways too and be ready to play when called upon."

Andy remembers the last time Leeds were promoted to the top flight in 1990, when he was in his early teens. "The whole scene took off then. The club has been a long time out of the top division this time around, so it would be nice to come full circle and see Leeds United back up there again," he said.

David Norris

13

Keeper Paddy wants a quick return to the Premier League

WHEN Paddy Kenny joined Leeds United from Queens Park Rangers in the summer it was the fourth time Neil Warnock had signed the Republic of Ireland international.

The pair share a mutual respect that stretches back to the days when they were together at Bury before joining up at Sheffield United, QPR and Leeds. They won promotion to the Premier League together at Sheffield United and QPR and are now looking to make it a hat-trick by taking Leeds into the top flight.

Warnock made no attempt to hide his admiration for Kenny when he said before the start of the 2012-13 season: "Paddy has always been the main man I've wanted to sign. I wouldn't swop him for any keeper in the Premier League or the Championship. He is the best keeper in the country."

That was quite a billing to live up to, but Paddy was quick to settle in at Elland Road and show the kind of form that made Warnock so keen to get him on board.

They say goalkeepers mature with age and Paddy can call on the experience of over 600 career appearances, including 33 Premier League starts in the 2011-12 campaign. Shot-stopping ability, safe handling from set-pieces, positioning sense, anticipation and ball distribution are

qualities all managers and coaches look for in a top goalkeeper and this guy has the lot.

Yet Halifax-born Paddy, 34, was once told by his home town club Halifax Town that he wouldn't make a goalkeeper because he was too small. They released him for that reason, but he has proved them wrong on countless occasions since.

He said: "You can imagine how upset I was at the time because I thought it might be the end of my career and at such an early stage. I just played locally, got a job as an engineer and then played part-time at Bradford Park Avenue, training a couple of nights a week and doing jobs during the day."

15

It was Warnock who rescued him from that tiring routine by signing him for Bury as understudy to Dean Kiely, who passed on a wealth of knowledge and advice. Paddy was loaned out to Whitby Town, where he gained more valuable experience which was to stand him in good stead. Although Bury were relegated, Warnock then signed him for Sheffield United where the keeper really blossomed and stayed for eight years, winning promotion to the Premier League in 2006 and playing in FA Cup and League Cup semi-finals.

In 2010, Warnock signed him for the third time as they linked up at QPR and there were more promotion celebrations in 2011. So it was no surprise when Warnock moved for the goalkeeper yet again in July, 2012, shipping out Andy Lonergan to Bolton later that month and bringing in Jamie Ashdown from Portsmouth to provide competition for the jersey.

Paddy, who would have been understudy to Robert Green, Mark Hughes' signing from West Ham, if he had stayed at QPR, said: "Once I had

spoken to Neil Warnock and heard his plans for the club I really wanted to come. Hopefully I can do for Leeds what I did at QPR and help them into the Premier League where they belong.

"I am from around here and a lot of my family and friends are big Leeds United fans. It's one of the biggest clubs around and I want to show what I can do. Neil Warnock knows what he will get from me and I know what I will get from him. His record at this level for promotions speaks for itself. He told me to come here, be myself and bring my experience to try and get the club promoted.

"It's a difficult league and you have to make your home games winnable, but the enthusiasm of the crowd is a huge bonus. I've had a bit of stick from them in the past but hopefully I can change their minds and do well for them."

Although he was born in Halifax, Paddy has won seven caps for the Republic of Ireland. Both his parents are of Irish descent and he made his debut for the Republic back in 2004, retiring from international football three years later with seven caps to his name.

Jason Pearce

Ex-Pompey brigade looking to a brighter future

WHEN Portsmouth defender Jason Pearce became Neil Warnock's first signing of the summer, Leeds United fans little suspected that three more players would make the same journey from Fratton Park to Elland Road before the 2012-13 season began.

Portsmouth's cash problems forced the south coast club to slash their wage bill and United took advantage by snapping up David Norris, Luke Varney and keeper Jamie Ashdown from Pompey.

So we asked Jason to tell us just what his three pals from Portsmouth are like as players and people.

All three were signed in July and Jason said of midfielder David Norris: "I met him when he moved from Ipswich to Portsmouth and off the pitch he is a lovely guy who is really down to earth and gets on with everyone. You can always approach him for a chat.

"On the pitch, he works so hard for the team, he's a fantastic player and a real asset to the side.

"Luke Varney is a match-winner and a great lad to have around the dressing room because he's so funny. He's the joker in the pack, but when you are one-to-one with him on a serious note he is a really top guy. You can talk to him about anything and he gets the balance right between hard work and fun.

"It is in his nature to be a fun guy. He's like a big kid really, so he's great to be around. You need people like him to create a good atmosphere in the changing room. On the field he will be an important player for us this season and he has a lot of goals in him.

"Jamie Ashdown is another top guy who came to the club to push Paddy Kenny for the goalkeeper's shirt. Jamie is a very good shot-stopper so it will be interesting to see how things work out. It is a difficult job for him because Paddy is a top keeper, but he will work very hard to keep Paddy on his toes."

Michael Brown, another former Portsmouth player, moved to Elland Road a year earlier and had just left Fratton Park when Jason started his second spell there, but the pair quickly formed a friendship when Jason completed his transfer to Leeds. "Brownie's experience will be a big factor for us this year. I was really pleased when he signed another contract here," said Jason.

So is there a danger that the ex-Portsmouth brigade will keep themselves to themselves and not mix in with the rest of the squad? Jason is quick to rule out such a situation. "There is no Portsmouth clique in the dressing room," he insists. "Everyone gets on well. David, Luke and Jamie weren't here when I first arrived but the lads who were here gave me a big welcome and I felt at home straightaway. They have been brilliant, to be fair.

"Obviously, the Portsmouth lads get on after being together for a year or so, but we are all in it together, looking to do well for the team."

Having introduced his ex-Portsmouth colleagues, what does Jason have to say about himself? "I think everyone who knows me realises I gave 100 per cent for Portsmouth, but it was the right time for me to move on to help the club financially. I started out there as an apprentice before going to Bournemouth and then moving back again.

"After coming through the ranks at Portsmouth I just wanted to see the club do well."

There were reports that Jason was in tears after the Middlesbrough game, when it seemed Pompey might go out of existence, but he said: "That wasn't true. Obviously I was feeling very down. I wear my heart on my sleeve but I did stop short of tears that day. It was sad to see what was happening to the club. The lads had given their all and without the ten points penalty we would have stayed up."

Neil Warnock is reported to have tried to sign Jason for Queens Park Rangers and then attempted to get him on loan at Leeds towards the end of last season, but Jason said: "That's the first I've heard about it. I genuinely

knew nothing about it at the time. I am a loyal person and did my best for Portsmouth, but it's nice to be wanted, of course, and I jumped at the chance when Leeds came in for me in the summer."

Warnock says of Jason: "He can be a bit naive at times and will make mistakes, but 99 per cent of the time you know what he is going to do – and he will do it well."

Jason responded: "That is a fair assessment. I made a mistake, for instance, in the Capital One Cup game against Shrewsbury. It was an honest mistake and nearly let their striker in, but I will learn from it and make sure it doesn't happen again. You have to learn very quickly because at this level it can cost you a goal, especially in my position. You are going to make the odd mistake. It is how you react that counts. We have good coaches here and you can't ask for anything more."

In April, 2012, Jason won seven of the nine available supporters' awards at Portsmouth, including Player of the Season, but all his loyalties are now with Leeds. "I did my best for Portsmouth when I was there and now I am here I will do the same for Leeds," he vowed.

Neil Redfearn

New Under- 21 league opens the way to a first team chance

DEVELOPMENT Squad Manager Neil Redfearn believes the new Under-21 League, introduced at the start of the 2012-13 season, is a big step in the right direction for bringing on young players.

Neil, who had a four-match spell in charge of the first team between Simon Grayson's sacking and Neil Warnock's arrival last February, plays a big part in equipping youngsters for the demands of senior football, and he is full of praise for the new league.

Behind closed doors friendlies replaced reserve games at the club last season but the new league has re-introduced a competitive edge. Neil explained: "Last season we were not in a reserve league. We just played friendlies and it worked to our advantage because we were able to play high profile games against the likes of Chelsea and Celtic.

"You don't know what you are going into until it starts, but the new league has produced some really high quality games. They are very close to a first team tempo and the technical ability is there. The rules state that you are only allowed to play four seniors and one of them has to be a goalkeeper. The gaffer decides which seniors to play and I try to play to a system as close as possible to the one the first team plays. Naturally, there are games where we don't have the personnel to play that system so we have to look at something a bit different. As part of their development the kids have to feel comfortable doing the things the first team are doing.

"It is an on-going progression from being scholars to young pros and your elite kids can get into that group pretty quickly. Obviously you are mindful of their age and if they can cope physically or not. If they tick the boxes the benefits of being in the group are unbelievable. I looked at our bench for an Under-21 game against Nottingham Forest and all of them were second year scholars. Two of them came on and changed the game, which bodes really well."

Eight pros were taken into the Development Squad after an outstanding season as Under-18s when they finished runners-up to Newcastle, though Neil rated the Leeds lads the best in that league.

United fans were able to see at first hand the progress made by youngsters Sam Byram and Dominic Poleon, who made their first team debuts at the start of the 2012-13 campaign. Sam's goal in the Capital One Cup 3-0 win over Oxford at Elland Road was extra special and Neil said: "He got away from two defenders, kept his cool and chipped the keeper. Sam has a very senior outlook. He is a baby-faced assassin who still looks about 13, but he has the maturity of a seasoned pro.

"Sam and Dominic know they have an experienced manager in Neil Warnock who is brave enough to put them into the first team and give them a chance. That bravery sometimes gets rewarded, as it has been with those two."

Redfearn welcomes the competitive nature of the new league and says: "The kids are at that age where a winning mentality is so important. It makes the move from Under-21 level into the first team that much easier for them if they are in a competitive environment and understand how it works."

Crazy mixed up United

Here are six members of the United squad but somehow their heads have all got mixed up. Can you sort them out and work out which part goes with which?

Answers on page 63.

1

a
b
c

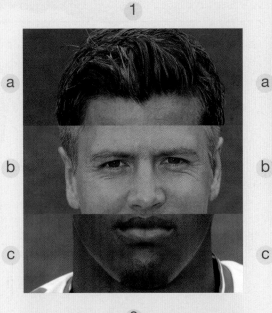

2

a
b
c

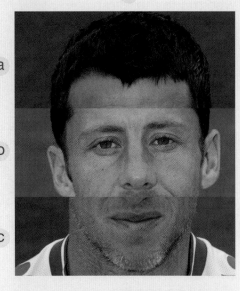

3

a
b
c

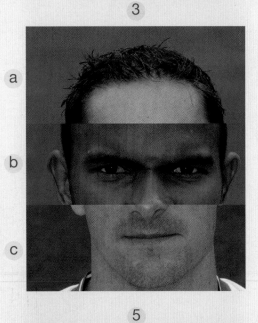

4

a
b
c

5

a
b
c

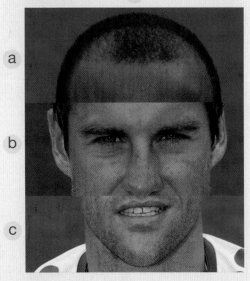

6

a
b
c

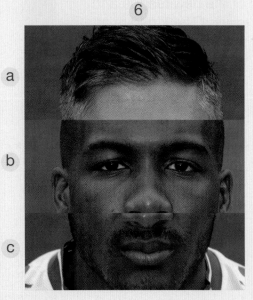

Luke Varney

23

Physio Harvey has a crucial role to play

WHEN a footballer gets injured it's vital that he receives the best possible treatment. So Leeds United's Head Physio, Harvey Sharman, has one of the most important jobs at the club.

Publicity-shy Harvey stays well out of the limelight and 'Mr Modesty' took a lot of persuading to do this interview. Yet his dedication to the job comes over loud and clear as he talks about the satisfaction he gets from helping players with serious and minor injuries back to full fitness.

"You take real pride in getting players back from injury into the first team because that's your job," says Harvey. "You build up close relationships with these guys because you spend so much time with them and just want to see them right. It becomes a personal thing."

No-one has spent more time being treated by Harvey than United's Australian defender Paddy Kisnorbo, who suffered an Achilles tendon injury in March, 2010, that kept him out until the final game of the following season. Then he damaged a knee at home to Burnley in January, 2012, and was sidelined for the rest of that season.

Paddy had warm praise for Harvey in an article that appeared in last year's Leeds United Annual. The admiration is mutual and Harvey says: "Paddy has been so unfortunate picking up serious injuries. If it had happened to anyone else I would have questioned whether they would have fought their way back.

"The lad has a special mentality. He is a tough kid and I think it is the Aussie in him. He just won't take 'no' for an answer. He wants to push himself all the time, so sometimes you have to say to him 'whoa – steady on'. You couldn't work with a better athlete in terms of the effort he gives."

Elsewhere in this Annual, Leigh Bromby talks about the excellent treatment he received when he suffered a snapped kneecap tendon at Cardiff last April. Harvey was quickly on the scene to comfort the player and tend to his injury. "To start with, you make him comfortable, reduce the pain and make sure he is stable," he said. "The medical treatment Leigh received at Cardiff was superb – from the orthopaedic surgeon to the paramedics etc.

"The next process is to get the right man to do the surgery – someone with a lot of experience in that field. The player has a massive input into that. Then it is down to us to start his rehabilitation. It is a lengthy process, but the facilities at this club are superb. We have everything we could ask for and we are constantly

reading up on the latest techniques, information and research."

Harvey took a change of direction in his career to become a physio. He had studied civil engineering at university but didn't enjoy it much. He injured a medial ligament playing football for Salts Old Boys, in the West Riding County Amateur League, and it was while being treated for the injury that he developed an interest in physiotherapy.

Harvey had always fancied working in football, but he needed to gain the right qualifications to become a physio, arriving at Elland Road after jobs at Oldham and Blackburn Rovers. He worked under highly respected physio Dave Hancock for a short time at Blackburn and spent four or five years under him at Leeds before taking over as Head Physio when Dave left for Chelsea.

"I learned a huge amount from Dave Hancock. When he left here he asked me to go to Chelsea too, but the opportunity to run on my own two feet at Leeds was too good to miss," said Harvey, who has never regretted his decision.

Promotion favourite

LEFT BACK Adam Drury is too modest to mention it, but before joining Leeds United in the summer he won a place in Norwich City's Hall of Fame after 11 years at Carrow Road.

Adam had two spells in the Premier League there and won back-to-back promotions to the top flight – experience that will stand him in good stead as he strives to help Leeds back into the elite as well.

One of the biggest disappointments of the summer for Leeds fans was the departure of crowd favourite Robert Snodgrass to Norwich, following in the footsteps of Jonny Howson, who had switched from Elland Road to Carrow Road in January.

Yet it wasn't all one-way traffic as Adam travelled in the opposite direction to join United's new-look squad under Neil Warnock. The defender, who had twice been appointed the Canaries' captain by Nigel Worthington, decided to end his long association with the club when his latest contract ran out.

"I was delighted when Leeds came in for me because it was a great opportunity," said Adam who began his career at Peterborough before signing for Norwich and being voted the club's Player of the Year in 2002-3.

"I met the gaffer, heard what he had to say and jumped at the chance. I was lucky enough to win those back-to-back promotions to the Premier League with Norwich and I would love to go up again, this time with Leeds, which is why I've come here.

"I had a great time at Norwich, where the promotions were the highlight, especially the one when I was captain.

Some players go through a whole career without getting promoted, so you really enjoy promotions when they come along. But in football, as in life generally, all good things come to an end. Coming to Leeds offers an exciting new challenge, so hopefully I can create some good memories here."

Warnock revealed that he pestered Adam's agent for years in the hope of signing him, but without success until the lure of Leeds proved too tempting. Adam said: "I don't know why it never happened until now. Neil did tell me about it when I came here, but he didn't tell me at the time! I've played against a few of the gaffer's teams and I know how he works and what he is all about.

"Obviously that is one of the reasons I decided to come here. He 'sold' the club to me – not that it needed any 'selling'. What you see is what you get with Neil Warnock. He tells you what he wants from you and if you don't do it you don't play – simple as that. He gets the best out of players, has been successful and you know where you stand with him. Every player appreciates that honesty in a manager.

"He has mentioned that he wants the outright record of eight promotions before retiring. That is his drive and motivation. He has put together a squad of players who know what this league is about, so hopefully we will be in the mix."

With Aidy White rejecting the chance to move on and deciding to sign a new contract instead, Adam finds himself in competition with the local boy for the left back role, though Aidy can operate

down the left flank as well. Competition for places is nothing new to Adam, who lost his place at Norwich to Marc Tierney last season before winning it back for a game against Tottenham at Carrow Road in December with Tierney injured.

Adam also suffered serious knee problems, which caused him to miss most of the 2007-8 and 2008-9 seasons, but he fought back from those to regain full fitness and continue where he left off. And before completing his move to Leeds, the Norwich public turned out in force to pay their tribute at a testimonial match between the Canaries and Celtic, which Norwich won 2-0.

Leigh setting his sights on a record recovery

ASK any footballer what he fears most in his career, apart from being cast aside by his club, and the answer comes flying back: a serious injury.

For defender Leigh Bromby, April 21, 2012, is a date that holds horrendous and painful memories. Yet the man who suffered one of the game's rarest injuries during a 1-1 draw at Cardiff in Leeds United's last away game of the 2011-12 season, is looking on the positive side.

And he is determined to become the first professional footballer to play again after suffering a ruptured patella tendon, just under half an hour into that fateful game in South Wales.

Not that Leigh is likely to be back in the first team before the end of the 2012-13 season, but he is hoping to play for the club at some level before next summer arrives.

His determination and optimistic approach is an example for any footballer to follow, and he is grateful to the medical experts who have done so much to rebuild both his knee and his confidence for the future.

Leigh said: "They don't know much about the injury because, as far as I am aware, there is only Matt Murray, who used to play for Wolves, who has had the same problem and he had to retire. But you wouldn't believe the work done on my knee by Andy Williams, the surgeon in London, and I am pleased with how things are going.

"I know I am going to be out of action for a long time. They said 12 to 18 months at the time and, as someone said, if I had been a racehorse they would have put me down! It has taken a bit of getting my head round, but I am over the worst now and there are a lot of targets to aim at."

Leigh added: "It was an unfortunate time for me to get the injury because it looked like I was just getting back into the first team picture again. It was my third successive game in the side and the injury was a real shock. At the time, I thought I'd broken my leg. I looked around and there was no-one near me. The pain was terrible and I knew straightaway that it was serious.

"The way Cardiff dealt with it was fantastic. The kneecap had come away and was in my thigh, so they had to manipulate it back. They had a knee and trauma specialist on hand and I will always be grateful for that, so I wrote them a letter thanking them for the way they dealt with it. They got my parents over and I couldn't have asked for any more from them."

Cardiff has long been a jinx ground for United, who went into that match in April without a win there since 1984. "I suppose if I was going to get a serious injury it was going to be there, but I have nothing but praise for the care I received that day," said Leigh who is also thankful for the countless hours spent on him by Harvey Sharman and his fellow physios at Thorp Arch.

"I am focussing really hard on the rehab stuff. The facilities we have here are second to none and the physios are top quality. I work with Harvey every day and when you are injured you are in from nine to five, so they work you hard. It's been quite a shock really."

Dewsbury-born Leigh, 32, has some sound advice for any youngster unfortunate enough to suffer a major injury on the way to making it as a professional footballer. He says: "I'm a bit older than that, but I would advise any young player to stay positive if he gets injured. They have to remember they have time on their side.

"I know how frustrating it is to sit out so many games when your team-mates are out there playing, but all the hard work on the way back to fitness will be worthwhile. I had a lot of growing pains when I was growing up and it is worrying at the time but, as I said, you have to remain positive if you pick up a serious injury.

"I am looking forward to getting back running again and training maybe some time after Christmas. The lads have been very encouraging and it's good to have the banter with them, but there's nothing like playing. That's what you miss the most."

When Celtic turned Ross away for being too small!

WHEN Ross McCormack was growing up as a kid on the south side of Glasgow he always looked forward with special excitement to Christmas and birthdays because that usually meant a new football would be among his presents.

Like most of his pals, Ross would spend most of his spare time kicking a ball around in the street and he was soon showing enough promise to play for his local boys club and try his luck at Celtic. Unfortunately, Celtic told him he was too small and turned him away.

That rejection could have put him off the idea of a career in football but instead it made him all the more determined to prove Celtic wrong. And as luck would have it, the manager of his boys club team went to manage Rangers' under-10s, took him with him and Ross was back on track to become a professional footballer.

He started out in Rangers' youth team in 2002 and went on to make 11 first team appearances and score two goals before being loaned out to Doncaster and then released by Rangers whose new manager Paul Le Guen said he didn't figure in his plans. Ross then joined Motherwell, where he scored ten goals in 48 games, before netting 25 goals in 74 games for Cardiff, forming a strong partnership with Jay Bothroyd.

He moved to Elland Road in 2010 and finished the 2011-12 season as United's top scorer with 19 goals, 18 of them in the Championship. Yet Ross wasn't always a forward. "I played in central midfield until I was about 15," he revealed. "Then I played up front in one game, scored four or five goals and stayed in that position. I had always chipped in with a few goals from midfield and enjoyed that too."

Ross added: "I was happy with my goals total last season because in the two seasons before that I hadn't played much. This season it will probably be a bit more difficult to reach that tally of 19 goals from the position I am playing in

because I'll be too busy trying to create goals. I am not bothered, so long as I am helping the team.

"Luciano Becchio will mainly stay inside the box and I will look to create things for him. I don't mind if he gets 20 goals and I set them up for him. I am happy with that. You are not going to score goals all the time, that's for sure. You have to have more to your game – just look at the goals Messi and Ronaldo set up, as well as scoring themselves. Their link-up play is so important."

For much of last summer it seemed Ross would be on the move, but a new contract was eventually agreed, much to his delight. "When nothing was agreed at the end of last season I thought I was going to be sold," he said. "Then I came back in pre-season and the gaffer said he had changed his mind. Under no circumstances was he going to let me go and they needed me to sign a new contract. It got sorted and I was delighted.

"I never wanted to leave, because you are not going to get any better facilities or supporters than we have here. It would have been hard going to another club, but when the time comes you have to look after yourself, like Robert Snodgrass did when he went to Norwich. Robert had a good few years here and did well. He felt the time was right to move on and that was up to him. It's good to play with him for Scotland and we room together when we are away on international duty."

Ross is optimistic about United's chances this season. He says: "The team has a strong spine with Paddy Kenny in goal, Tom Lees and Jason Pearce at the back, then Rodolph Austin in midfield and me and Luciano up front. Of course we will get injuries and suspensions and it's not a massive squad but we do have good players."

Muddled Managers

UNJUMBLE these letters to spell the names of ten Leeds United managers. To help you we have given you some clues and the answers are on Page 63

WIDAOKNSHRHLWOI

Took United to promotion from the old Second Division in 1990 and to the League Championship in 1992.

EYEBNRTSRVEAL

Former England manager whose initials are TV and is often seen on TV!

ERDIEOVN

Spent 13 years in charge at Elland Road and was the club's most successful manager.

KAONINRLEWC

Has seven promotions to his name and is looking for an outright record eighth.

MILRFJYFMAEDI

This former England captain succeeded Brian Clough as Leeds manager.

GULNRCBAIOH

Enjoyed great success in the game but not at Leeds where he lasted just 44 days in the job.

NAYGIORSOMNS

Took Leeds to promotion from League One to the Championship and took over at Huddersfield Town after losing his job at Elland Road.

NITJKOSCE

Hugely successful Celtic manager, who also managed Scotland. Left Leeds after 45 days in charge.

EADREDGYI

Very popular member of Don Revie's 'Super Leeds' team. Appointed the club's player-manager in 1982 and caretaker-manager when Peter Reid left in 2003.

SIDNENWSIE

Not very tall but a Chelsea and Wimbledon legend. Left his job at Leeds in 2008 to become Executive Director at Newcastle United. His surname means wisdom.

34

Answers on page 63.

Statue tribute to our greatest manager

LEEDS UNITED supporters turned out in their thousands on Saturday May 5, 2012, to pay tribute to the late Don Revie, whose bronze statue was unveiled outside the ground by members of the club's 1972 FA Cup winning team.

Legends from the Revie era, including Allan Clarke, Mick Jones, Johnny Giles, Norman Hunter, Eddie Gray, Peter Lorimer and Paul Reaney, admired the £90,000 bronze statue, watched by Don's son Duncan, daughter Kim and other family members.

The ceremony took place 40 years after Leeds' FA Cup triumph over Arsenal in Wembley's Centenary Final.

Don, who died of motor neurone disease in May, 1989, aged 61, was the most successful manager in Leeds' history during his 13 years in charge, before leaving in 1974 to take the England job as Sir Alf Ramsey's successor.

Clarke, scorer of the goal that sank Arsenal at Wembley in 1972, said: "Don built one of the greatest football teams this country has seen and will ever see.

"As our captain Billy Bremner always said, 'The gaffer was Leeds United and we players were his disciples.'"

Duncan Revie, who bears a striking resemblance to Don, said the statue was a great honour and tribute to his father "and that wonderful team."

The statue, sculpted by Graham Ibbeson, from Barnsley, is located on Lowfields Road, opposite Elland Road's East Stand and just a stone's throw from a similar tribute to the late Billy Bremner, who is generally regarded as the greatest captain in United's history.

Among other notables whose statues have been sculpted by Graham are Fred Trueman, Harold 'Dickie' Bird and Eric Morecambe.

Michael Brown

Question & Answer

EXPERIENCED midfielder Michael Brown agreed a new one-year contract in the summer. We asked him a host of questions to find out more about the Hartlepool-born man who has also played for Portsmouth, Wigan, Fulham, Tottenham, Sheffield United, Hartlepool and his first club Manchester City.

Question: Who was your football hero as a boy and why?
Answer: I liked Paul Gascoigne a lot. I remember him playing for Tottenham and being a wizard. He had character and personality and of course he was an amazing player. I remember him coming to Hartlepool with Tottenham. I was at the game and looked for him especially. I loved watching Liverpool as a kid too.
Q: Who is the best player you have played with and why?
A: I would have to say Georgi Kinkladze. He was an incredible player. He had everything. If you tried to kick him he would just bounce off you. He could take the ball in any tight situation and could have gone on to be a world superstar, but it never worked out for him. The year he had at Manchester City was fantastic.
Q: What is your biggest achievement in football so far?
A: To have played for so many clubs and still be playing football at 35. I've had some great days and thoroughly enjoyed my career at lots of clubs. The 2010 Cup Final was mega against Chelsea, even though Portsmouth lost

1-0. Another memorable game was beating Tottenham to reach the Cup Final at Wembley when no-one gave Portsmouth a prayer because there was a chance they were going out of business. Hearing the deafening noise from Portsmouth's fans was something else. There were special games with Sheffield United, too, when we beat Liverpool and one that no-one really mentions when we beat Nottingham Forest 4-3 in a play-off semi-final second leg to go through to Cardiff.
Q: Apart from sport, what was your best subject at school?
A: Definitely maths – basic numbers, not deep mathematic theories. Give me numbers and I'm quite quick.
Q: If you hadn't been a footballer what would you have done for a living?
A: I would probably have been selling something, but I don't know what.
Q: What is your biggest disappointment in football?
A: It has become very cut-throat. It is big

business and there is always someone wanting to fill your shoes and shove you aside if they can. I am talking in general terms now. It's still enjoyable, but when the focus was more on football being a sport, everyone was a bit more relaxed and easy-going.

Q: *Who has had the biggest influence on your career and why?*

A: My Missus because she stops me going to the pub! I can't say that can I? Seriously, my dad and granddad have been the biggest influence. They were there for me from the start. My dad has probably been to nearly every game I've played as a pro. He played non-league and since he's stopped playing he's been everywhere to watch me, which is good. My granddad took me to play in matches at weekends when I was a kid because dad was playing at the time, but since I started as a pro, dad has travelled many thousands of miles to watch me. He never missed a Portsmouth home game and he's from Hartlepool! If the team was in London he'd be on the train first thing on a Saturday morning and before he retired he would take Wednesday mornings off after going to Tuesday night games.

Q: *What advice would you give to a talented youngster hoping to make a career in football?*

A: First and foremost you've got to enjoy it. If you are not enjoying it you are not going to make it, because the modern game is very serious and very professional. You have to enjoy what you do. I think they take it too seriously too early these days. You have to be as fit as you can be or you will be left behind.

Q: *What are your own strengths and weaknesses?*

A: Eating ketchup is very much a strength! More seriously, I am a team player and help to win the ball back. Now I am getting older I can help as an organiser and give a little bit back to the team. Maybe I would like to score more goals because it's great when you do. I scored one against Forest last season and until then I hadn't scored for quite a while. It's not really important to me because if I am in the opposition's penalty box I think our team is vulnerable.

Q: *Have you always played in midfield?*

A: I played striker until I was about 17 and loved it. In the youth team I was a striker but gradually moved back into midfield. I scored lots of goals as a kid. I suppose everybody did.

Q: *Who did you most admire at the 2012 Olympics and why?*

A: Mo Farah winning the gold medal in the 5,000 metres. That was some race. Where he found that extra energy to burst through and win after putting so much effort into his run I don't know. He must have done so much work in training to be able to do that. All our medal winners were amazing and there were so many from Yorkshire.

Q: *Some people have said footballers can learn from Olympic athletes when it comes to being down to earth and modest about their achievements. Do you agree?*

A: There are some footballers with bad images and some who create an image that will get them into the papers and make them even bigger names, but most of the lads are down to earth and just enjoy playing football. When kids at 17, 18 or 19 have lots of money, fame and attention it can be very tough to handle, so I admire those who keep their feet on the ground, as the majority do.

Q: *What has been your worst injury and how long did it keep you out?*

A: I damaged my left ankle when I was about 18 and it took me five months. It was very frustrating but, touch wood, I've been very fortunate to avoid serious injuries considering how many games I've played. You have to remember that when you do get a knock there is always somebody worse off than you like Leigh Bromby, who had an horrendous injury.

You have your little niggles here and there and just hope the worst injuries don't happen to you.

Q: *Have you ever regretted becoming a footballer?*

A: Never. Not one bit. When each season starts and you walk out into that great atmosphere, even if you are on the bench, as I am likely to be, you think 'this is why I became a footballer'. The first day of the season is always special for me.

Q: *When your career is over would you fancy going into coaching or management?*

A: Yes I would but I am not 100 per cent sure in what capacity or where. I have to do some badges first. I will be looking into that.

Q: *Do you have any superstitions?*

A: Yes. I always go out last if I'm not captain. It's something I've always done. If I can, I always stop for a cup of tea and a muffin before home games. I've done that for years. The sugar gives me a nice bit of energy and it's good to relax with that muffin and tea. Weird or what!

Q: *What irritates you most about people inside or outside football?*

A: People who are a bit sneaky or who tell lies when they don't have to. I don't like people to be unreliable.

Q: *Are you a good timekeeper?*

A: When you travel a lot, as I do as a footballer, you have to be on time. I would rather be ten minutes early than ten minutes late arriving at the ground. If I have a hairdressing appointment, say at four o'clock, I try to be on time. I wouldn't turn up at quarter-past.

Q: *Does anybody else in your family play football?*

A: My dad did and my little boy, who is two, is starting to kick a ball about a lot, so we'll see.

Q: *What is your biggest ambition left in football?*

A: To play as many games as I can at as high a level as I can for as long as I can.

How hopes rose, only to fall...

Tom Lees makes his first league start against Middlesbrough.

UNITED'S second successive season of Championship football began disappointingly, gained momentum and then faded into a mid-table finish. A leaky defence and a club record 11 home defeats were largely to blame for the failure to capture a place in the play-offs and manager Simon Grayson paid for the lack of success by losing his job at the start of February, with United in tenth place.

After Neil Redfearn was briefly placed in temporary charge, Neil Warnock took Grayson's place but it soon became clear that the man who boasted a joint record seven successive promotions would have to wait at least one more season if he was to take the record outright.

August

United lost on the opening day for the second successive season, going down 3-1 at Southampton where they trailed by three goals before Max Gradel fired home an injury-time consolation from the penalty spot. There were league debuts for defender Daniel O'Dea, keeper Andy Lonergan and midfield man Michael Brown.

With Gradel, O'Dea, Robert Snodgrass and Aidy White on international duty, United entertained neighbours Bradford City in the Carling Cup first round and, despite trailing twice, came through to win 3-2. Ramon Nunez scored twice and Ross McCormack netted the first of his 19 goals for the season as United maintained their record of never losing against City at Elland Road in a major competition.

Young defender Tom Lees was handed his first league start in an eventful home game against Middlesbrough which saw the visitors win 1-0 against a Leeds side reduced to nine men. United had lost Max Gradel and Jonny Howson – both sent off for receiving two yellow cards – by the time Marvin Emnes scored the decisive goal in the 67th minute. Zac Thompson left the bench for his Leeds debut and although Boro had been reduced to ten men when Tony McMahon received his second yellow card in first half injury-time, United's nine men couldn't find an equaliser.

Tom Lees will long remember United's first win league of the season, against Hull City. He scored for both

Luciano Becchio returns to head in against Palace.

sides, including his first goal for the club, in a 4-1 home win. Ross McCormack opened the scoring, Tom's own-goal gifted Hull a 21st minute equaliser but the youngster was overjoyed to equalise and further goals from Robert Snodgrass and Leigh Bromby sent United fans home happy. Andy Keogh made his debut on his return to the club on loan from Wolves.

A visit to West Ham, who were to finish in third spot, saw United twice hit back to share the points, but there was another own-goal, this time from Patrick Kisnorbo just two minutes after Ross McCormack had cancelled out Carlton Cole's sixth minute opener for the Hammers. Adam Clayton struck United's late equaliser with his first goal for the club.

Ramon Nunez, who had scored twice against Bradford in the Carling Cup first round, collected another brace in Round Two as Doncaster Rovers were beaten 2-1 at the Keepmoat where James Hayter caused a scare by finding

United's net as early as the second minute. Zac Thompson marked his first start with a win.

The month ended as it had started – with an away defeat. Aidy White was sent off in the 48th minute of a 2-1 reverse at Ipswich. Ross McCormack gave United a first half lead but late goals from Jason Scotland and Keith Andrews denied the ten men and left them in 19th place.

September
Luciano Becchio, who had been out of action with a hamstring injury since April, made a goal-scoring comeback in a 3-2 home success against Crystal Palace. Ross McCormack struck at the double and there were debuts for 17-year-old defender Charlie Taylor and Finland striker Mikael Forssell.

Ross McCormack's seventh goal in nine games sealed a 2-1 home victory over Bristol City. Adam Clayton struck for United after only three minutes but Neil Kilkenny produced a spectacular equaliser against his old club. Patrick Kisnorbo was sent off in the 65th minute for conceding a penalty but Andy Lonergan saved Nicky Maynard's spot-kick and McCormack's goal four minutes from time settled matters.

Manchester United's arrival at Elland Road in the Carling Cup third round raised pre-match excitement but three first half goals without reply saw Sir Alex Ferguson's men through. Michael Owen scored the first two on a rare first team appearance and Ryan Giggs added the third.

The month ended with a 3-3 draw at Gus Poyet's Brighton – United's first visit to the Amex Stadium. Danny Pugh made his debut a second time around, having rejoined the club from Stoke, initially on loan. Andy Keogh and Ross McCormack built a two-goal lead but then trailed before McCormack struck again in added time to rescue a point. Grayson criticised the defence for switching off at vital times.

October
The opening day of October brought United's first clean sheet of the campaign and a 1-0 home win over troubled Portsmouth, Danny Pugh's 14th minute header proving sufficient. Danny was on target again when United followed their Carling Cup win at Doncaster in August with a 3-0 league victory at the same venue – their first away league win of the season. Ross McCormack and Tom Lees were the other scorers in Simon Grayson's 150th game in charge. Keeper Andy Lonergan fractured a finger and was replaced by Paul Rachubka who started the next five matches.

Darren O'Dea's first goal for the club looked like giving United a home win over Coventry but the Sky Blues' Leeds fan Richard Wood equalised three minutes into added time, courtesy of Rachubka's mistake. A third win in four games saw United temporarily climb

into third place as they returned from Peterborough with a 3-2 success. Peterborough's Lee Tomlin was sent off in the 37th minute and Darren O'Dea's winner, off the under-side of the bar, came five minutes into added time.

A seven-match unbeaten league run ended with a single goal defeat at Birmingham – the first time United had failed to score on their travels this season. They hadn't beaten Cardiff at Elland Road since 1983 and had to settle for a point this time, Robert Snodgrass netting a 70th minute equaliser.

November
Keeper Paul Rachubka had a nightmare against his old club Blackpool who emerged 5-0 winners. Blackpool cashed in on three first half mistakes by Rachubka who was replaced at half-time by young debutant Alex Cairns. Tom Lees was sent off for handling during a mix-up with Rachubka that led to a penalty.

Not surprisingly, Rachubka was dropped and never played for the first team again, spending loan spells at Tranmere and Orient during the season. Alex McCarthy was signed on loan from Reading and played his part in a much-needed 1-0 home win over manager-less Leicester. Adam Clayton's superb strike into the top corner settled a game of few chances for United's first win over the Foxes in nine attempts.

The recovery continued with a 2-1 win at Burnley where Robert Snodgrass scored two late goals. United defender Andy O'Brien, who it later transpired had been suffering from acute depression, refused to be selected. The mini-revival ended with Barnsley's first victory at Elland Road for 22 years. Ross McCormack had the consolation of ending his seven-match goal famine with a free-kick.

The visit to Nottingham Forest was overshadowed by news 48 hours earlier that former Leeds and Wales international Gary Speed had committed suicide. United dedicated their 4-0 win to Gary.

December
A 2-0 home win against Millwall in an early kick-off saw United briefly climb into fourth place but there was little cheer during the rest of December as the month yielded just three points from a possible 15. Tributes were paid to the late Gary Speed at the game against Millwall and Robert Snodgrass scored from a free-kick and a rare header to give United their first home win since October 1.

Alex McCarthy saved a penalty from Marvin Sordell in a 1-1 draw at Watford where Robert Snodgrass was on target from the spot four minutes into added time. Then came successive defeats at home to Reading and away to Derby and Barnsley. Keeper Andy Lonergan returned from injury against Reading who registered their first ever league win at Elland Road with Simon Church's second minute goal.

A second half goal by Jamie Ward sentenced United to defeat at Derby's Pride Park and Ricardo Vaz Te's hat-trick helped Barnsley to a comprehensive 4-1 win at Oakwell. Craig Davies also scored and all United could muster was a late goal from substitute Luciano Becchio. Simon Grayson described his team's performance as "totally unacceptable" and warned some players had played their last game for the club.

January
A 2-1 home win against ten-man Burnley probably saved Grayson's job – for the time being anyway! Ross McCormack's winner arrived five minutes into injury time. Burnley's Kieran Trippier was sent off for his second bookable offence with just half an hour gone. Andros Townsend, on

Thierry Henry celebrates as Leeds fall out of the FA Cup at the Emirates.

loan from Tottenham, made his Leeds debut and unlucky Patrick Kisnorbo was ruled out for the rest of the season with a knee injury.

The FA Cup third round saw United knocked out by Arsenal for the second year running but once again Grayson's men gave a commendable performance at the Emirates. However, instead of gaining an Elland Road replay this time they fell to a memorable goal from Arsenal legend Thierry Henry, who was on loan from New York Red Bulls.

Robert Snodgrass, back after an appendix operation, left the bench to equalise and earn a point at Crystal Palace who had Sean Scannell sent off just before half-time for his second yellow card. For the third successive league game United saw an opponent sent off as they recorded a 3-1 win at home to Ipswich. This time it was former Leeds keeper Alex McCarthy, on loan to Ipswich from Reading, who saw red for handling outside his area in the 71st minute. Andy Drury had put Ipswich ahead in the 34th minute but United, with Fabian Delph back at the club on

Simon Grayson's last match in charge was against Birmimgham in January.

Neil Warnock took over on February 18.

loan from Aston Villa, took full advantage of McCarthy's dismissal with goals by Robert Snodgrass, Ross McCormack and Luciano Becchio.

Simon Grayson's last match in charge saw United humiliated by giant Serbian striker Nicola Zigic, who scored all Birmingham's goals in a 4-1 rout at Elland Road after Ross McCormack had opened the scoring. Grayson and his first team coaching staff were sacked the next day (February 1).

February

Neil Redfearn was placed in temporary charge and his prospects of landing the job permanently received an initial boost from a 3-0 win at Bristol City, though the home side had two players sent off. Right back Adam Smith made his debut for United on loan from Spurs and goals came from Robert Snodgrass, Ross McCormack and Luciano Becchio.

Successive 2-1 defeats against Brighton and Coventry wrecked any chance Redfearn had of succeeding Grayson, especially as Coventry were

bottom of the table. Gary McSheffrey rifled in two penalties for the Sky Blues.

Neil Warnock, most people's favourite to take over from Grayson, was appointed before United took on Doncaster at Elland Road on Saturday, February 18, and although he wasn't due to take full charge until the Monday, he gave an inspirational pep half-time talk with the side trailing 1-0. Warnock's words had the desired effect and United ran out 3-2 winners. Andros Townsend, Adam Clayton and Luciano Becchio scored the Leeds goals, Becchio's winner arriving just before the end.

With Warnock at the helm, United recorded their first goalless draw of the season, watched by a sell-out crowd of 17,571, at Portsmouth.

March

By now, United's play-off hopes were fading fast and when high-flying Southampton came to Elland Road for a teatime game screened by Sky, the Whites' luck was well and truly out. Ricky Lambert scored from the Saints' only menacing attack, Kelvin Davis was inspired in the visitors' goal and United hit the woodwork three times. Danny Webber, who had joined the club as a free-agent, having left Portsmouth, made his debut as a substitute.

Webber made his first start in a goalless draw at Hull where Andy Lonergan pulled off some excellent saves. Robert Snodgrass scored United's first goal since Warnock took full charge with the opener in a 2-0 win at Middlesbrough, Luciano Becchio adding the second and defender Paul Robinson making his debut on loan from Bolton.

Elland Road's biggest crowd of the season – 33,366 – turned up to see West Ham scrape a 1-1 draw with a late equaliser from Danny Collins after Luciano Becchio had headed United in front, but a big shock was just around the corner. Nottingham Forest chopped Leeds down to size with an amazing 7-3 triumph. It was the first time United had conceded seven goals at home and Garath McCleary bagged four of them. Michael Brown's goal was his first for Leeds but Warnock said he was embarrassed by the result, adding that some of the defending was "Sunday League standard."

Although they sat in tenth place, United were just three points away from a play-off place after bouncing back with a 1-0 win at Millwall where Ross McCormack scored and Andy Lonergan saved a penalty from Darius Henderson. However, after a 2-0 defeat at home to Watford, in which Paul Connolly was sent off, Warnock confessed that the squad needed major surgery.

April

United lost by the same score at champions-elect Reading, where Zac Thompson was sent off after only 12 minutes and home substitute Adam Le Fondre scored twice after leaving the bench. United's discipline was deserting them and Michael Brown was ordered off in another 2-0 defeat, this time at home to Derby on Easter Monday. By now United had slid into 14th place.

Neil Warnock's first home win since taking total charge arrived against Peterborough who were thrashed 4-1 despite taking a 38th minute lead through Joe Newell. Billy Paynter, given a rare start in United's attack, scored twice and Ross McCormack's brace took his total for the season to 19.

Darren O'Dea became the fourth Leeds player to be sent off in the last five games as United lost 1-0 at Blackpool and the gloom showed no sign of ending when Leigh Bromby suffered a snapped kneecap tendon in a 1-1 draw at Cardiff, Luciano Becchio scoring with a 73rd minute header.

The final game of the season, at home to Leicester was a dead rubber. Danny Webber left the bench to equalise with his first goal for Leeds who justifiably claimed Harry Panayiotou's injury-time winner was offside.

United finished in 14th place, leaving Neil Warnock much to think about over the summer months.

Billy Paynter celebrates scoring against Peterborough.

Have you been paying attention?

Last year we ran a quiz to test your Leeds United knowledge, with all the answers to be found by reading the Annual. It proved so popular that we have decided to run a similar quiz this year. Once again there are some pictures to help you. How many can you get right without looking up the answers?

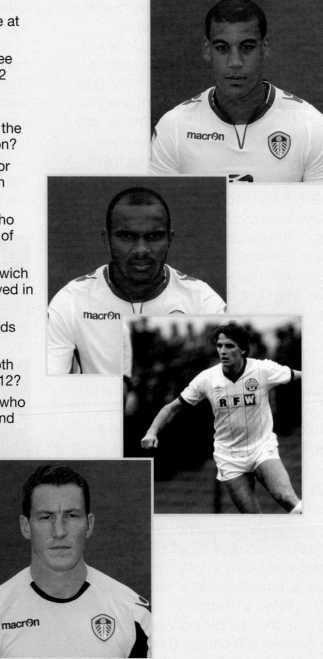

1. Who did Michael Brown most admire at the last Olympics?

2. Leigh Bromby suffered a serious knee injury towards the end of the 2011-12 season. Which team was he playing against at the time?

3. Who did Neil Warnock choose to be the club's captain for the 2012-13 season?

4. Which team did Jason Pearce play for before rejoining Portsmouth and then signing for Leeds?

5. Who is the Jamaican international who joined Leeds United from SK Brann, of Norway?

6. Robert Snodgrass left Leeds for Norwich in the summer of 2012, but who moved in the opposite direction?

7. Andy Gray's dad also played for Leeds United. What is his name?

8. Which Leeds defender scored for both sides against Hull City in August, 2012?

9. What is the name of the goalkeeper who signed for Leeds from Portsmouth and started the season as understudy to Paddy Kenny?

10. Who is Leeds United's Head Physio?

Answers on page 63.

Sam Byram

47

Lee Peltier

48

ASK Lee Peltier to name the highlights of his career so far in football and back comes the unhesitating answer: "Being made captain of Leeds United and playing in the Champions League for Liverpool."

Pelts, as he is known in the dressing room, could not have been more pleased when Neil Warnock asked him to take on the captaincy two weeks after the versatile defender was signed from Leicester City in August.

After all, there were plenty of other players at the club who had worn the captain's armband at their former clubs, but Warnock saw the qualities in Peltier that made him ideal for the job. The manager said at the time: "He has all the attributes to be captain of a great club. I've watched him cajole and talk to the players and organise them. It was a gut feeling to hand him the captaincy. He's a nice lad off the field, and on it he is respected by the players."

Lee said he was "absolutely buzzing" to be given the role, adding "it was a proud moment for me and my family. I was surprised because a few of the lads have had experience of captaining other clubs and I came here late, but I wasn't going to turn it down! It's a real privilege."

Liverpool-born Peltier felt similar pride when he played for his home town club against Turkish club Galatasaray in the Champions League, but any hopes he had of building a long career at Anfield were dashed as he found the way to a regular first team place blocked.

"It was a long time ago and I was there at the wrong time," Lee explained. "There were so many good players who didn't get a chance under Rafael Benitez. I was loaned out to Hull City for a while and didn't make a league appearance for Liverpool before joining Yeovil.

"Benitez had his own thoughts and ways. When I was there he preferred foreign players. Then, when I had just left, they started pushing young lads through!"

It was a case of bad timing, but Pelts made a name for himself at Yeovil where he played 69 league games before joining Huddersfield Town, Leicester and Leeds. He rates himself a late entrant into football as he was ten years old before taking a keen interest in the game.

Lee takes up the story: "I was always into athletics and tennis but when we moved house I was new in the street and a couple of lads knocked on the door asking if I wanted to join them in a game of football, so I did. I really enjoyed it and I've never looked back since."

Pelts may have been born in Liverpool but he knows all about Yorkshire after his two seasons at Huddersfield where he suffered play-off heartbreak twice. "Although I was happy at Huddersfield it was disappointing that I didn't get promoted with them, so after those two years I decided to try the Championship and when Leicester came in for me it was hard to say no," he said.

Soon after signing Pelts for Leeds, Warnock said: "He has the makings of a top player but in my opinion he has been wasted over the last 12 months. He can go as far as he wants in the game."

Lee disagrees that he was wasted at Leicester, because he played a lot of games for them, but he feels Warnock will get the best out of him. "I was happy at Leicester but then certain things made me unhappy. There was a change of manager (Nigel Pearson took over) and things didn't work out. He wanted to bring in his own sort of players and play to his own style, which is fair enough.

"He didn't say I wasn't part of his plans but we did have a chat and decided it would be better for me to move on."

Warnock stepped up his interest in Pelts after failing to sign Joel Ward from Portsmouth, and Leeds beat off competition from Huddersfield Town who were keen to re-sign him. Although he arrived at Elland Road as a right back, he showed his versatility by filling three different positions in his first three league games for the club – operating at centre back against Wolves, left back at Blackpool and right back at Peterborough.

Lee has no objections about that and says: "I don't mind at all. I will play anywhere the gaffer wants me to play and always give 100 per cent. Obviously my preferred position is right back but I will do a job for the team wherever it might be. I've played a lot of games in midfield in the past too. If you are good at football you should be able to adapt and I rate it a bonus that I can play in different positions. It is good for the team if I am needed in a different area of the pitch

"Kids tend to start out in one position but don't always end up there. A lot of strikers end up as wingers, for instance, or central midfielders finish up as centre backs – that sort of thing. The coach will soon tell you where he thinks you can make a career, so my advice to youngsters would be to listen and take on board whatever advice they are given about the best position to fill."

Peltier is not a Liverpool name, of course. His dad's side of the family is from the Caribbean and he has French ancestry, but Lee played for England at Under-18 level. "It has been a short career up to now but I've enjoyed every second of it," he beams. "I just hope I can keep progressing, along with the club. My main ambition is to win promotion with Leeds and I think we can do it. I wouldn't have joined them if I thought otherwise."

Third time lucky

WHEN Rodolph Austin signed for Leeds United in the summer it was a case of third time lucky for the Jamaican international who was bursting to play in English football.

Stoke City were keen to sign the midfielder or defender in 2008 but a work permit appeal failed and when Neil Warnock tried to snap him up after trials at Queens Park Rangers in 2011, SK Brann, of Norway, scuppered the move because their valuation of the player was more than the Londoners were prepared to pay.

So the quietly spoken Rodolph was highly delighted when Warnock came in for him again, this time as manager of Leeds United who succeeded in getting him a work permit and agreeing a fee.

Rodolph, whose mentor at Brann was the former Leeds and Norway international midfielder Eirik Bakke, isn't complaining about having to wait so long for a transfer to an English club. He isn't the sort to let things get him down and says: "Although I was disappointed when I didn't go to Stoke I believe everything happens for a reason and I live my life like that.

"You can't go around complaining, because you never know what may be waiting around the corner. When I went back to Norway I worked even harder at SK Brann and did well over there. When Neil Warnock wanted me at QPR, Brann were asking a lot of money and wouldn't let me go. I didn't question it because it is funny the way things turn out in football. Sometimes it is not the right time or the right place.

"I am here at Leeds now and I feel it is the right time and the right place. The manager has got his man at last, I am enjoying it at Leeds and I am determined to do my best."

One of the main reasons Rodolph wanted to play in England was to test himself at a different level with a big club. He said: "I was very pleased when I heard Leeds United were interested because they are a very big club with wonderful supporters. I had heard good things from past players, including Erik Bakke, and knew all about the atmosphere the big crowds create here.

"I really enjoy playing in front of big crowds. When the ground is full for an international match in Jamaica the crowd is about 35,000 and the fans over there make a lot of noise, so I am used to that."

Rodolph twice won the Caribbean Cup with Jamaica and in 2010 was named the most valuable player in the competition. He started out as a defender and can still play at the back, though for most of his career he has played in midfield and enjoys it there. "I have always admired Steven Gerrard and John Barnes," he says. "John is Jamaican and, like Gerrard, played for Liverpool, of course, but there are lots of players I have tried to learn from by watching them and playing against them.

"As a Jamaican player I have always looked up to Ricardo Fuller too. I know him well and he is a good man."

Rodolph's biggest influence at Brann

was Bakke who was such a favourite with the fans during his time at Elland Road. "Eirik was a very good person to me and an excellent player," he beamed. "To play in the same team as him was special. He gave me a lot of advice, telling me what I was doing wrong and motivating me as well. When I was alone and bored in hotels at Brann he took me to restaurants where we would just sit, eat and talk a lot. He really tried to make me feel at home and I have been made to feel very welcome here at Leeds too.

"The fans are really enthusiastic and I just want to repay them by doing my best out there on the pitch. If a tackle is there to be made I will make it because I like to win and help the team in the best way I can. I know I am not the type of player to go past five or six opponents, but I like to win the ball and pass it."

So what does Rodolph make of Neil Warnock as a manager now he is part of the former QPR boss's squad? "He is a straight-up guy who can be funny and make you laugh," he says. "He will shout at you today and then come in tomorrow and pat you on the back, so you know what he wants from you. I am learning a lot from him and all the coaches at Leeds and I want to keep improving all the time."

Agony and ecstacy as United lift Cup

NO FAN old enough to remember Leeds United's one and only FA Cup Final triumph will ever forget the unbridled joy that accompanied the 1-0 victory over Arsenal in the 1972 Centenary Final, at Wembley.

The Gunners may be gloating over their third round 1-0 win against us at Highbury in January, 2012, when Thierry Henry left the bench to score that memorable and decisive goal, but last May's 40th anniversary of our Wembley success brought memories of the big day flooding back.

Allan Clarke wrote his name into Leeds United folklore with the stooping header that sent the Cup to Elland Road and atoned for previous Cup Final defeats to Liverpool in 1965 and Chelsea in 1970.

Clarke, the willowy striker who had cost manager Don Revie a then British record £165,000 from Leicester City in June, 1969, was the hero of the hour, but one of the abiding memories of that day was the bravery of Allan's co-striker

Mick Jones.

Mick, who had set up the goal with a determined run and pinpoint cross from the right, suffered the excrutiating pain of a dislocated elbow but, watched by millions on TV, he somehow summoned the courage to clamber up the steps to the royal box and collect his winner's medal, with his damaged arm in a sling.

Mick wasn't going to miss out on

receiving his medal from The Queen, and his courage was hailed at the time by Dr Andrew Stephen, chairman of the Football Association at the post-match banquet in London.

The players had to miss the banquet because they were cruelly made by the Football League to play a title decider at Wolverhampton on the Monday night, but Dr Stephen told his audience: "We were all sorry about the injury to Mick Jones. The determination of that young man to come up for the presentation was very much noted and appreciated."

In the players' absence the banquet was described by club president Lord Harewood as "Hamlet without the prince."

And club chairman Ald Percy Woodward summed up many people's feelings when he said: "The FA Cup is the most coveted trophy on this earth. My one regret is that the boys who have won and earned it are not here at this celebration."

The first half of the final was a dour affair, containing too many fouls for the purists' liking, but once Clarke's 53rd minute header had billowed the net, Arsenal had to come out of their shell and the match improved as a spectacle.

United had lost a lead to Chelsea in the 1970 final but Jack Charlton and the magnificent Norman Hunter bolted the door at the back, leaving Arsenal's attack powerless to make a breakthrough.

Revie's Super Leeds team had many superstitions and when they were held up in traffic on their way to Wembley they spotted a bride on her way to church. Immediately they took that as a good omen, as they had so often been 'bridesmaids' in big matches. Now they were to be the bride!

Clarke said: "That bride was the best mascot we could have had."

Yet as one journalist wrote at the time: "With respect, Leeds didn't need a mascot, rabbit's foot or anything else. They had all it took to win this one and with better finishing the margin of victory would have been greater."

Unfortunately, United failed to complete the coveted double as Wolves were 2-1 winners at Molineux on the Monday night, making Derby County the champions. Referee Bill Gow somehow failed to award Leeds a penalty when TV cameras clearly showed Wolves defender Shaw bouncing the ball with BOTH hands!

But no-one could take away the memory of that FA Cup triumph two days earlier when a jubilant Billy Bremner raised the trophy aloft.

Colourful
FOUR

THESE four Leeds United players make a colourful bunch when you know their surnames. Who are they? Answers on page 63.

Paul's hoping the grass is Greener at Elland Road

MIDFIELDER Paul Green couldn't believe his bad luck when he injured a knee on his league debut for Leeds United against Wolves at Elland Road on the opening day of the 2012-13 Championship season.

Signed from Derby County, where he had spent four years, the Pontefract-born Republic of Ireland midfielder had impressed in pre-season and then played his part in the 4-0 trouncing of Shrewsbury Town in the first round of the Capital Cup.

The injury was a blow to Green and manager Neil Warnock, especially as the player was hoping for an injury-free introduction to life at Elland Road, having proved his fitness at Derby after battling back from a cruciate medial ligament injury suffered while playing for the Rams against Cardiff in 2011.

In March, 2009, he broke a metatarsal in training which put him out for the rest of that season. He needed pain-killing injections when he returned to action and then required an operation on his foot. Yet Paul still managed to chalk up 143 games for Derby before rejecting a contract offer and moving to Elland Road, a transfer that delighted his wife Claire, who has long been a staunch Leeds fan.

"Coming from Pontefract, I have a lot of friends who are Leeds supporters," said Paul, who played against his present club for Doncaster

in the 2008 League One play-off and finished on the winning side. So, in hindsight, does he now wish Leeds had beaten Doncaster that day and won promotion?

"You can't think that way," he replies. "You just want to win for the team you are playing for at the time and no-one wants to lose at Wembley or anywhere else."

Paul made his debut for Doncaster at the age of 19, in 2002, enjoying three promotions with them. He rose from the Conference through to the Championship, winning the Football League Trophy and gaining valuable experience along the way. He scored 33

goals in 277 games for Doncaster before being snapped up for Derby by Paul Jewell and was delighted when Leeds gave him the opportunity to return to his Yorkshire roots.

Derby thought so highly of him that when Celtic showed interest during the 2009-10 season, the Rams management described him as "untouchable". And before Paul left for Leeds, Derby manager Nigel Clough praised his loyalty by declaring: "When there have been so many departures and so much upheaval in the last few years, I think it is a huge compliment to him that he stayed here for so long."

But the lure of playing at Elland Road proved too strong for Paul who had enjoyed playing under Clough but was eager to accept the new challenge.

"I had some great times at Derby and the fans were fantastic to me," said Paul. "It came down to a fresh challenge. I sat down with my family and discussed it and reached the decision that it was time for a change."

He qualifies to play for the Republic of Ireland through his grandfather on his mother's side and was delighted to make an appearance in Euro 2012 when he came on as a substitute against Spain. "That was an unbelievable experience. There are players who never get to play in the European Championships, so I was well pleased," he said.

So he was on a high as he entered a new season as a Leeds United player, only for that knee injury to cause a frustrating spell on the sidelines. Fortunately, it was no-where near as serious as the one he endured at Derby and he is full of optimism about the future at Elland Road.

"I needed no convincing about coming to Leeds," he said. "You only have to look at what Neil Warnock has done with other clubs to get them into the Premiership and that is where I want to be."

Quicksilver White chose football over athletics

IF Aidy White hadn't been a footballer, the fleet-footed left back or winger would probably have taken up athletics.

He was outstanding at both when he attended St Mary's School, Menston, and during the summer he was glued to his television set, watching the Olympics.

The Brownlee brothers and Lizzie Armitstead live close by in Bramhope and Otley, respectively, and Aidy has nothing but admiration for their medal-winning efforts.

Sport was and still is greatly encouraged at St Mary's and as well as his exploits on the football field, Aidy excelled at the 100 metres and the long jump.

Yet it was while he was still a primary school pupil that he first found a passion for football. Uncles and cousins played for a team called Menston Hotshots and Aidy joined them when he was about five or six years old. "There wasn't a team in my age group at the time so I had to play against boys a year older," he recalls. "My brother is two years older than me so I played in his team as well.

"Then, when I was eight or nine, Leeds United scouted me. There were big trials for Under-8s and Under-9s and I was taken on, so I've been here for something like 12 years. Maybe I'll be in line for a testimonial soon," he laughed.

Aidy lives so near to St Mary's School that he goes back there if he needs to do a bit of extra training on their all-weather pitch. "The facilities at the school are very good. They've just got a new pitch and it's fantastic. If I ever want to use it I nip over the road for a bit of practice."

Aidy has kept in close touch with his teachers at St Mary's and appreciates the encouragement they gave him during his time as a pupil there. "I go back every now and again to see a few of the teachers and we talk on the phone too. I do miss it," he says. "All the PT teachers there encouraged me a lot but Mr Geldart was my mentor."

Aidy is renowned for his lightning pace, which helps him to create chances and get back rapidly in defence when needed. "I've always been quick," he says. "I don't know where it comes from. My dad says it's from him, but when I give him a race he gets nowhere near me! I used to win the sprints at school and had a fond interest in athletics.

"I really enjoyed the 100 metres and long jump, but there comes a time when you have to dedicate yourself to one sport and for me it was always going to be football. That didn't stop me from following the Olympics, though. I thought the whole thing was fantastic and seeing people live their dreams was really special."

The dedication shown by the Olympians is closely matched by the support Aidy has received from his parents. "Mum and dad have dedicated pretty much all their lives to me, running

around after me," he says with genuine appreciation. "Dad would take me anywhere to play, whether it was down south, up north or abroad. Sometimes I would be training six nights a week, and every night he would be there.

"I can't thank him enough so I have to try and repay him by playing well. I am sure he feels the pressure up in the stands. I know I don't like watching a mate or a family member playing either."

Aidy's fans were delighted when he signed a new contract in the summer of 2012 after it seemed he may be on his way out of Elland Road. I wanted to stay straightaway but it took about ten months to sort out, which seemed forever," he said. "It was a bit of a nightmare but I finally got it sorted and I'm glad I did."

Like some of his Leeds team-mates, Aidy qualifies to play for the Republic of Ireland through grandparents on his dad's side from Wexford. He had already played for England's Under-19s but hadn't been selected for a while when the Irish asked if he would be interested in playing for them and he immediately said yes.

"I have Irish blood in me so I couldn't turn down the opportunity," he said. "It helps your career when you are given the chance to play international football."

Aidy is always being asked whether he will settle down at left back or on the wing, and he's still not sure. "Neil Warnock might see me as a winger. He has told me that and I have no problems with it. Other managers have played me at left back or on the wing but when I started out I was pretty much a left back and that is where I always played through the Academy," he said.

"I don't really mind and I don't know which position I am better at, so it is a difficult one. We'll just have to wait and see. What I do know is that I'll have to fight for a first team place because although it's a small squad it is a strong one. I think we are capable of doing brilliant things."